Let Us Have Music for Piano

Seventy Four Famous Melodies

ARRANGED AND EDITED BY MAXWELL ECKSTEIN

CARL FISCHER ®

62 Cooper Square, New York, NY 10003

Copyright © 1940 by Carl Fischer, Inc., New York
International Copyright Secured
Printed in U.S.A.

O3127

0 8258 0048 X

FOREWORD

These volumes have been prepared with the following points in view:

1. For adults or children who have a limited technique, and are in the early grades of piano playing.

2. For study and recreational purposes.

3. For sight reading.

The compositions herein are too difficult in their original form to be played by persons whose technical development is immature. They have therefore been carefully arranged in the easier keys, within the average vocal range, and are suitable for singing if desired, lyrics having been included with most of them. They have been edited to meet a specific need for elementary piano material.

We feel certain that this book will prove a valuable addition to the repertories of all who wish to make the music hour a pleasant one.

Maxwell Eckstein

ALPHABETICAL INDEX

Classified Index on Page 112

Hail, Columbia!

Hail, Columbia, happy land!
Hail, ye heroes, heav'n-born band!
Who fought and bled in Freedom's cause,
And when the storm of war was gone,
Enjoyed the peace your valor won.
Let independence be our boast,
Ever mindful what it cost;
Ever grateful for the prize,
Let its altar reach the skies.

Refrain:
Firm, united let us be,
Rallying 'round our liberty;
As a band of brothers joined,
Peace and safety we shall find.

PHILIP PHILE (?)
Arranged by Maxwell Eckstein

03127
29288-98

Columbia, The Gem of the Ocean

O Columbia, the gem of the ocean,
The home of the brave and the free,
The shrine of each patriot's devotion,
A world offers homage to thee.
Thy mandates make heroes assemble
When Liberty's form stands in view;
Thy banners make tyranny tremble,
When borne by the red, white and blue.

Refrain
When borne by the red, white and blue,
When borne by the red, white and blue,
Thy banners make tyranny tremble,
When borne by the red, white and blue.

Thomas à Becket

Arranged by Maxwell Eckstein

When Johnny Comes Marching Home

When Johnny comes marching home again, Hurrah! Hurrah!
We'll give him a hearty welcome then, Hurrah! Hurrah!
The men will cheer, the boys will shout,
The ladies, they will all turn out,
And we'll all feel gay
When Johnny comes marching home.

PATRICK S. GILMORE
Arranged by Maxwell Eckstein

Red River Valley

From this valley they say you are going,
I shall miss your sweet face and your smile;
Just because you are weary and tired
You are changing your range for a while.

Refrain
Then come sit here a while ere you leave us,
Do not hasten to bid us adieu;
Just remember the Red River valley,
And the cowboy who loved you so true.

Cowboy Song
Arranged by Maxwell Eckstein

Billy Boy

Oh, where have you been, Billy boy, Billy boy,
Where have you been, charming Billy?
I've been to seek a wife,
She's the joy of my life.
She's a young thing and cannot leave her mother.

American Folk-Song
Arranged by Maxwell Eckstein

Jingle Bells

Jingle bells! Jingle bells!
Jingle all the way!
Oh, what fun it is to ride
In a one-horse open sleigh!

Traditional
Arranged by Maxwell Eckstein

Grandfather's Clock

My grandfather's clock was too large for the shelf,
So it stood ninety years on the floor.
It was taller by half than the old man himself,
Though it weighed not a pennyweight more.
It was bought on the morn of the day he was born,
And was always his treasure and pride;
But it stopped short, never to go again
When the old man died.

Refrain
Ninety years without slumbering,
    Tick, tock, tick, tock,
His life seconds numbering
    Tick, tock, tick, tock,
It stopped short, never to go again
When the old man died.

HENRY C. WORK (1832–1884)
Arranged by Maxwell Eckstein

The Man on the Flying Trapeze

Once I was happy, but now I'm forlorn
Like an old coat that is tattered and torn;
I'm left in this wide world to fret and to mourn,
Betrayed by a maid in her teens.
Now this girl that I loved, she was handsome,
And I tried all I knew her to please,
But I never could please her a quarter as well
As the man on the flying trapeze. Whoa!

Refrain

He flies through the air with the greatest of ease,
This daring young man on the flying trapeze,
His movements are graceful, all girls he does please,
And my love he's purloined away.

Arranged by Maxwell Eckstein

When You and I Were Young, Maggie

I wandered to-day to the hill, Maggie,
To watch the scene below,
The creek and the old rusty mill, Maggie,
Where we sat in the long, long ago.
The green grove is gone from the hill, Maggie,
Where first the daisies sprung;
The old rusty mill is still, Maggie,
Since you and I were young.

George W. Johnson

J. A. BUTTERFIELD (1837–1891)
Arranged by Maxwell Eckstein

Sweet and Low

Sweet and low, sweet and low,
Wind of the western sea;
Low, low, breathe and blow,
Wind of the western sea.
Over the rolling waters go,
Come from the dying moon, and blow;
Blow him again to me,
While my little one, while my pretty one sleeps.

JOSEPH BARNBY (1838–1896)
Arranged by Maxwell Eckstein

Massa's in de Cold, Cold Ground

'Round de meadows am a-ringing
De darkies' mournful song,
While de mocking bird am singing,
Happy as de day am long.

Refrain
Down in de corn field
Hear dat mournful sound;
All de darkies am a-weeping,
Massa's in de cold, cold ground.

STEPHEN C. FOSTER (1826–1864)
Arranged by Maxwell Eckstein

Camptown Races

De Camptown ladies sing dis song:
    Doodah, doodah;
De Camptown race-track five miles long,
    Oh, doodahday
I come down dar wid my hat caved in,
    Doodah, doodah;
I go back home wid a pocket full o' tin,
    Oh, doodahday.

Refrain
Gwine to run all night,
Gwine to run all day.
I'll bet my money on de bob-tail nag,
Somebody bet on de bay.

STEPHEN C. FOSTER (1826–1864)
Arranged by Maxwell Eckstein

Deep River

Deep river, my home is over Jordan,
Deep river, Lord, I want to cross over into camp ground.
Oh, don't you want to go to that gospel feast,
That promised land where all is peace?

Negro Spiritual
Arranged by Maxwell Eckstein

Nobody Knows De Trouble I've Seen

Nobody knows de trouble I've seen,
Nobody knows but Jesus.
Nobody knows de trouble I've seen,
Glory, Hallelujah!

Sometimes I'm up, sometimes I'm down,
Oh, yes, Lord.
Sometimes I'm almost to the groun'
Oh, yes, Lord.

I never shall forget that day.
Oh, yes, Lord.
When Jesus washed my sins away,
Oh, yes, Lord.

Negro Spiritual
Arranged by Maxwell Eckstein

Good Night, Ladies

Good night, ladies!
Good night, ladies!
Good night, ladies!
We're going to leave you now.

Refrain
Merrily we roll along,
Roll along, roll along,
Merrily we roll along,
O'er the dark blue sea.

College Song
Arranged by Maxwell Eckstein

For He's a Jolly Good Fellow

For he's a jolly good fellow,
For he's a jolly good fellow,
For he's a jolly good fellow,
Which nobody can deny!

Traditional
Arranged by Maxwell Eckstein

There Is a Tavern in the Town

There is a tavern in the town, in the town,
And there my true love sits him down, sits him down,
And drinks his wine mid laughter free,
And never, never thinks of me.

Refrain
Fare thee well, for I must leave thee,
Do not let this parting grieve thee,
And remember that the best of friends must part, must part.
Adieu, adieu, kind friends, adieu, adieu, adieu!
I can no longer stay with you, stay with you.
I'll hang my harp on a weeping willow tree,
And may the world go well with thee.

Old Cornish Air
Arranged by Maxwell Eckstein

The Minstrel Boy

The minstrel boy to the war is gone,
In the ranks of death you'll find him;
His father's sword he hath girded on,
And his wild harp slung behind him.
"Land of Song", said the warrior bard,
"Though all the world betray thee,
One sword, at least, thy rights shall guard,
One faithful harp shall praise thee."

Thomas Moore

Air: "The Moreen"
Arranged by Maxwell Eckstein

Flow Gently, Sweet Afton

Flow gently, sweet Afton, amang thy green braes,
Flow gently, I'll sing thee a song in thy praise.
My Mary's asleep by thy murmuring stream,
Flow gently, sweet Afton, disturb not her dream.
(*Robert Burns*)

Old Scottish Air "Afton Water"
Arranged by Maxwell Eckstein

A-Hunting We Will Go

A-hunting we will go,
A-hunting we will go,
Heigh-o the merry-o,
A-hunting we will go,
(Imitate bugles......)
A-hunting we will go.

Traditional
Arranged by Maxwell Eckstein

All Through The Night

Sleep, my child, and peace attend thee
All through the night;
Guardian angels God will send thee
All through the night.
Soft the drowsy hours are creeping
Hill and vale in slumber steeping,
I my loving vigil keeping
All through the night

Old Welsh

David Owen
Arranged by Maxwell Eckstein

Andante

29233-98

Sailor's Hornpipe

Arranged by *Maxwell Eckstein*

Shepherds Hey

Morris Dance

English Dance Tune
Arranged by Maxwell Eckstein

Come Back To Sorrento

Watch the sea so bright and lovely,
　Waking depths of tender feeling,
Like to you of whom I'm thinking
　Till I'm dreaming though awake.
See the lovely dewy garden,
　Breathing scent of orange blossoms;
Such a sweet and gracious perfume
　That it enters in one's heart.

Refrain
And you say,"Good bye, I'm going,"
　This poor heart of mine you're leaving,
Leaving this fair land of loving,
　Can you bear to not return?
Then leave me not,
　Nor give to me this torment,
Come back to Sorrento
　That I may live.
　　　　　(G. B. de Curtis)

E. de CURTIS (1875-1927)
Arranged by Maxwell Eckstein

Ciribiribin

A. **PESTALOZZA** (1851–1934)
Arranged by Maxwell Eckstein

La Paloma

We hoist our sails and gaily go to sea;
Oh, mother, now pray the Lord to watch o'er me.
     I saw 'neath the trees the maid who holds my heart,
"One word to comfort me, love, e'er we part."

And if at length the wild waves should claim their prey,
Seeking for thee, a white dove will come some day.
     Open thy casement, dearest, unto the dove,
For 'tis my soul that's seeking for thee, my love.

All ye sailors gay,
     Hoist your sails and away,
Leave care and sorrow; to-morrow
     We'll be up on the deep blue sea!

Alice Mattullath

S. YRADIER (1809–1885)
Arranged by Maxwell Eckstein

Santa Lucia

Now 'neath the silver moon, ocean is glowing,
O'er the calm billow soft winds are blowing;
    Here balmy breezes blow, pure joys invite us,
And as we gently row, all things delight us.

Refrain
Hark, how the sailor's cry
Joyously echoes nigh
    Santa Lucia! Santa Lucia!
Home of fair Poesy,
Realm of pure Harmony,
    Santa Lucia! Santa Lucia!
        (Anonymous)

Neopolitan Song
Arranged by Maxwell Eckstein

Alouette
(The Lark)

Alouette, gentile Alouette,
Alouette, Je te plumerai.
Je te plumerai la tete
Je te plumerai la tete
Et la tete, et la tete
Et la tete, et la tete, oh!
Alouette, gentile Alouette,
Alouette, Je te plumerai

French Canadian Folk-Song
Arranged by Maxwell Eckstein

Allegro

Mademoiselle from Armentieres
(Hinky Dinky Parlez Vous)

Mademoiselle from Armentieres, parlez vous?
Mademoiselle from Armentieres, parlez vous?
Mademoiselle from Armentieres,
You haven't been kissed in forty years,
Hinky dinky parlez vous.

Arranged by Maxwell Eckstein

Tempo di Marcia

Valse Triste

JEAN SIBELIUS (Born 1865)
Arranged by Maxwell Eckstein

Funeral March of a Marionette

CHARLES GOUNOD (1818–1893)
Arranged by Maxwell Eckstein

The March of the Three Kings
(Old French Christmas Carol)

From Provence
Arranged by Maxwell Eckstein

Minuet
from "Don Juan"

W. A. MOZART (1756-1791)
Arranged by Maxwell Eckstein

29233-98

Minuet

I. J. PADEREWSKI (1859-1941)
Arranged by Maxwell Eckstein

Minuet in G

L. van BEETHOVEN (1770 – 1827)
Arranged by Maxwell Eckstein

TRIO

Minuet D.C. senza replica

A Wandering Minstrel, I

from "The Mikado"

A wandering minstrel, I,
A thing of threads and patches,
Of ballads, songs and snatches
And dreamy lullaby.

My catalogue is long,
Through every passion ranging,
And to your humors changing
I time my supple song!

GILBERT and SULLIVAN
(1836 – 1911)   (1842 – 1900)
Arranged by Maxwell Eckstein

Allegretto con grazia

Berceuse
from "Jocelyn"

Oh, wake not yet from slumber's fold!
An angel fair thy dream is winging,
And, weaving thee a net of gold,
Thy dream's fulfilment may be bringing,
Sleep! Sleep! The day is not yet light!
Keep her, Mary, with thy blessed might!

Margarete Münsterberg

B. GODARD (1849–1895)
Arranged by Maxwell Eckstein

Andantino

Toreador Song
from "Carmen"

Toreador, on guard now!
Toreador, toreador!
And think that when in danger thou shalt be,
Dark eyes gaze and adore,
While true love waits for thee,
Toreador! Love waits, love waits for thee.

G. BIZET (1838-1875)
Arranged by Maxwell Eckstein

Allegro moderato

Song to the Evening Star
from "Tannhauser"

O thou sublime sweet evening star,
Oft I have greeted thee afar;
And if perchance she pass thee by,
Bring her my greeting beyond the sky,
When in the regions of the blest
Her soul has found eternal peace and rest.

RICHARD WAGNER (1813–1883)
Arranged by Maxwell Eckstein

Evening Prayer

from "Hänsel and Gretel"

When at night I go to sleep,
Fourteen angels watch do keep:
　　Two my head are guarding,
　　Two my feet are guiding,
Two are on my right hand,
Two are on my left hand,
　　Two who warmly cover,
　　Two who o'er me hover,
Two to whom 'tis given
To guide my steps to heaven.

E. HUMPERDINCK (1854-1921)
Arranged by Maxwell Eckstein

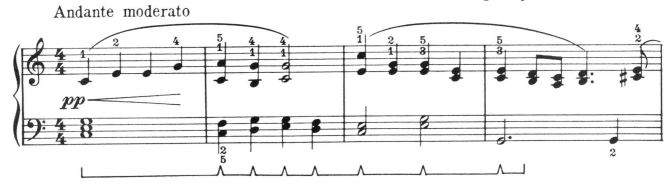

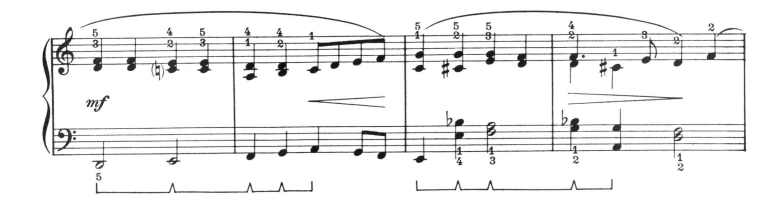

Pilgrims Chorus

from "Tannhauser"

Once more, dear home, I with rapture behold thee,
And greet the fields that so sweetly enfold thee;
Thou, pilgrim staff, may rest thee now,
Since I to heaven have fulfilled my vow.

By penance sore I have atoned,
And god's pure law my heart hath owned;
My pains hath he with blessing crowned,
To God my song shall aye resound.

Once more, dear home, I with rapture behold thee,
And greet the fields that so sweetly enfold thee;
Thou, pilgrim staff, thy toil is o'er,
I'll serve my God for evermore.

RICHARD WAGNER (1813–1883)
Arranged by Maxwell Eckstein

Andante maestoso

The Anvil Chorus

from

"IL TROVATORE"

G. VERDI (1813–1901)
Arranged by Maxwell Eckstein

Allegro

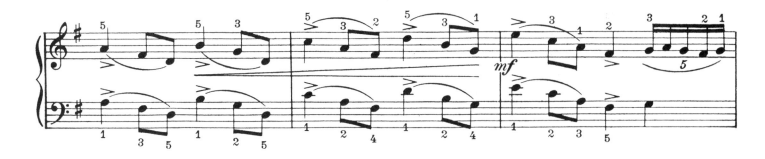

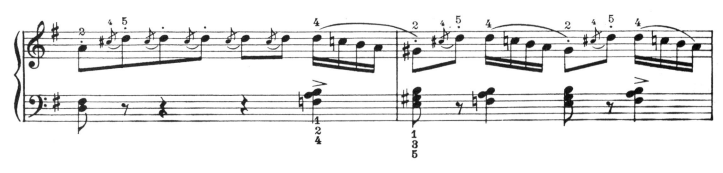

Brother, Come and Dance With Me

from "Hänsel and Gretel"

Brother, come and dance with me,
Both my hands I offer thee;
Right foot first, left foot then,
Round about and back again.

E. HUMPERDINCK (1854–1921)
Arranged by Maxwell Eckstein

Allegro

Vilia
from
"THE MERRY WIDOW"

FRANZ LEHAR (Born 1870)

Arranged by Maxwell Eckstein

29233-98

Triumphal March

from

"AIDA"

G. VERDI (1813–1901)
Arranged by Maxwell Eckstein

Barcarolle

from

"TALES of HOFFMANN"

Night of joy and ecstasy,
Be kind to every lover,
Fairer than the day to me,
O blissful night of love!

Time bears on relentlessly
The joys we ne'er recover,
Though in paradise we be,
Time flies eternally.

The zephyrs tenderly
O'er our happiness hover,
They sigh enviously
As they watch you and me.

Fairer far than the day, Ah!
Would that night never ended.
Night of joy,
O night of love!

Alice Mattullath

J. OFFENBACH (1819–1880)
Arranged by Maxwell Eckstein

Bridal Chorus
from
"LOHENGRIN"

Faithful and true, we lead ye forth,
Where love triumphant shall crown ye with joy!
Star of renown, flower of the earth,
Blest be ye both far from all life's annoy.

Champion victorious, go thou before,
Maid bright and glorious, go thou before!
Mirth's noisy revel ye've forsaken,
Tender delights for you now awaken!

Fragrant abode enshrine you in bliss,
Splendor and state in joy ye dismiss.

RICHARD WAGNER (1813–1883)
Arranged by Maxwell Eckstein

Oh! How So Fair

from

"MARTHA"

Oh! How so fair, Oh! So bright,
Burst her beauty on my sight.
Oh! So mild, so divine,
She beguiled this heart of mine.

Martha, Martha, thou hast taken
Every bliss away with thee!
Canst thou leave me thus forsaken?
Come and share thy boon with me!

F. von FLOTOW (1812–1883)
Arranged by Maxwell Eckstein

Then You'll Remember Me

from

"THE BOHEMIAN GIRL"

When other lips and other hearts
Their tales of love shall tell,
In language whose excess imparts
The power they feel so well.
There may, perhaps, in such a scene
Some recollection be,
Of days that have as happy been,
And you'll remember me.

W. W. BALFE (1808-1870)
Arranged by Maxwell Eckstein

Waltz

from
"FAUST"

C. GOUNOD (1818-1893)
Arranged by Maxwell Eckstein

Tempo di Valse

Hallelujah Chorus
from
THE MESSIAH

Hallelujah!
For the Lord God omnipotent reigneth.
The kingdom of this world
Is become the kingdom of our Lord
And of His Christ;
And He shall reign for ever and ever,
King of kings and Lord of lords.
Hallelujah!

GEORGE FREDERICK HANDEL(1685-1759)
Arranged by Maxwell Eckstein

Allegro moderato

Hark! The Herald Angels Sing

Hark! The herald angels sing,
"Glory to the new born king;
Peace on earth, and mercy mild;
God and sinners reconciled."
Joyful, all ye nations, rise,
Join the triumph of the skies;
With the angelic host proclaim,
"Christ is born in Bethlehem!"
Hark! The herald angels sing,
"Glory to the new born king."

Charles Wesley

F. MENDELSSOHN (1809-1847)
Arranged by Maxwell Eckstein

Abide With Me

Abide with me: fast fall the eventide,
The darkness deepens, Lord, with me abide!
When other helpers fail, and comforts flee,
Help of the helpless, O abide with me.

Henry F. Lyte

W. H. MONK (1823-1889)
Arranged by Maxwell Eckstein

EXCERPT
from
Danse Macabre

C. SAINT-SAËNS (1835-1921)
Arranged by Maxwell Eckstein

Allegro moderato

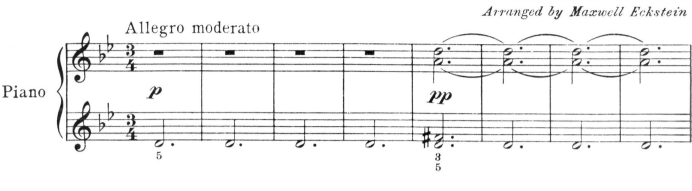

Piano

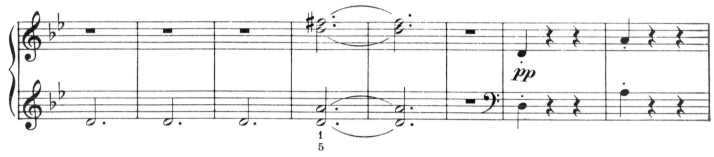

Tempo di Valse

Copyright 1942 by Carl Fischer, Inc., New York
International Copyright Secured

29226-3

29226-3

Amaryllis
Air Composed by King Louis XIII

HENRY GHYS
Arranged by Maxwell Eckstein

Allegro moderato

Largo

GEORGE FREDERICK HANDEL (1685-1759)

Arranged by Maxwell Eckstein

Two Grenadiers

To France were returning two grenadiers,
From Russia their way they were making,
And when they came to the German frontiers
Their hearts were depressed and aching.

'Twas there that they heard the sad story of woe:
The throne of their country was shaken,
Fair France had been conquered, her banners laid low,
And the Emp'ror a pris'ner was taken...... *(etc.)*

Alice Mattullath

ROBERT SCHUMANN (1810-1856)
Arranged by Maxwell Eckstein

Prelude in A Major

FREDERIC CHOPIN (1810-1849)
Arranged by Maxwell Eckstein

On Wings of Song

My wings of song uplifting,
I'll fly, my loved one, with thee
Where sacred waters are drifting,
The Ganges our goal shall be.

The moon shines on glowing red roses
That blossom everywhere,
The lotus flower uncloses
To greet her sister fair.

The violets nodding and bending
Are smiling to heaven above.
Softly the roses are blending
Their perfume with sighs of love.

The timid gazelles are bounding
To meet us from the wood,
A gentle murmur is sounding
Where rolls the sacred flood.

To rest then, in silence sinking,
Let us forget time's flight,
While peace and love we're drinking,
In dreams of endless delight.

Alice Mattullath

F. MENDELSSOHN (1809-1847)
Arranged by Maxwell Eckstein

Loch Lomond

By yon bonnie banks and by yon bonnie braes,
Where the sun shines bright on Loch Lomon',
Where I and my true love were ever wont to be,
On the bonnie, bonnie banks of Loch Lomon',

Refrain
Oh, ye'll tak' the high road and I'll tak' the low road,
And I'll be in Scotland afore ye;
But I and my true love will never meet again
On the bonnie, bonnie banks of Loch Lomon'.

Lady John Scott

Old Scottish Air
Arranged by Maxwell Eckstein

THEME
from
Rondo Alla Turca
(SONATA IN A MAJOR)

W. A. MOZART (1756-1791)
Arranged by Maxwell Eckstein

Allegretto

Largo
from the Symphony in E minor
"From the New World"

ANTON DVOŘÁK (1841-1904)
Arranged by Maxwell Eckstein

THEME
from
Symphony in G Major
(SURPRISE SYMPHONY)

JOSEPH HAYDN (1732-1809)
Arranged by Maxwell Eckstein

Andante

29238 - 98

THEME
from
Fifth Symphony

L. van BEETHOVEN (1770–1827)
Arranged by Maxwell Eckstein

Andante con moto

THEME
from

Finlandia

JEAN SIBELIUS (Born 1865)
Arranged by Maxwell Eckstein

THEME
from
"Romeo and Juliet"

P. I. **TSCHAIKOWSKY** (1840–1893)
Arranged by Maxwell Eckstein

THEME
from
Unfinished Symphony

FRANZ SCHUBERT (1797-1828)
Arranged by Maxwell Eckstein

Allegro moderato

Cortège du Sardar

from
CAUCASIAN SKETCHES

M. IPPOLITOV-IVANOV (1859-1935)
Arranged by Maxwell Eckstein

Allegro moderato (Marziale)

THEME
from
Piano Concerto No.1

P. I. TSCHAIKOWSKY
Arranged by Maxwell Eckstein

Andante non troppo

Piano

f maestoso   *mf*

Ped. simile

Ped. simile

29205-2

Copyright 1941 by Carl Fischer, Inc., New York

CLASSIFIED INDEX